Mel Bay Pres:

ACCORDION
Music from
Around the World

By Frank Zucco

1 2 3 4 5 6 7 8 9 0

© 1993 by Mel Bay Publications, Inc., Pacific, MO. 63069.
All Rights Reserved. International Copyright Secured. B.M.I. Made and Printed in the U.S.A.

CONTENTS

España

4

5

Amerika-Rossiya
America Russia

Russian

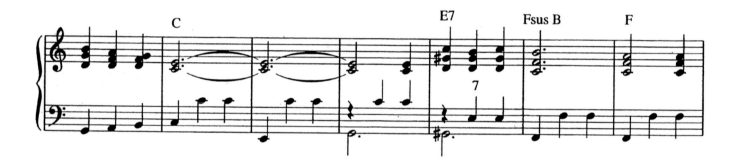

Used by permission

Tamo Daleko

So Far Away

Serbia

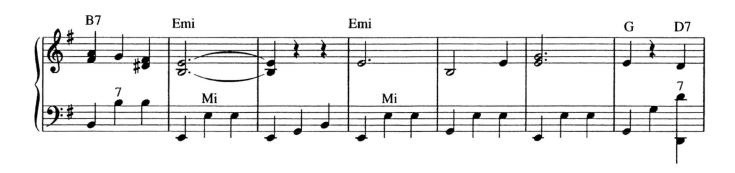

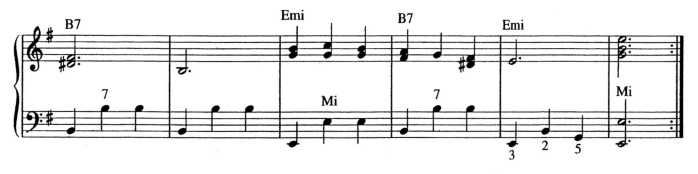

Värssyjä Sieltä Ja Täältä

Here and There

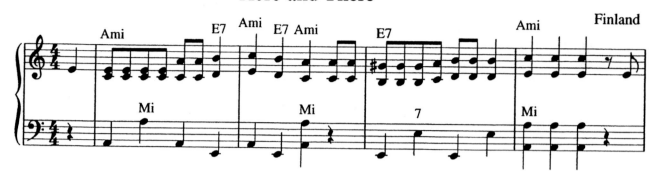

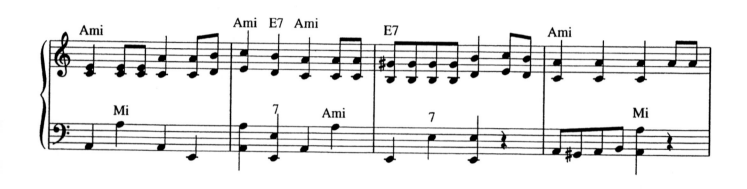

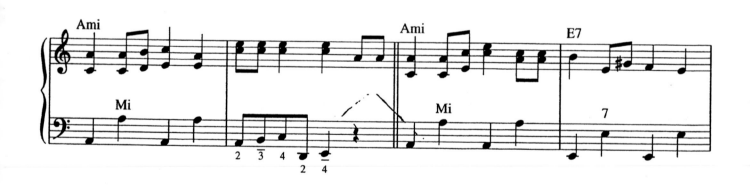

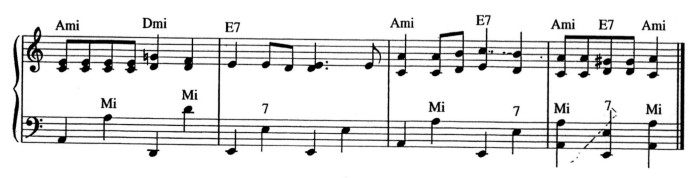

Gu Ma Slan Do Na Fearaibh

Here's Good Health to the Heroes

Scotland

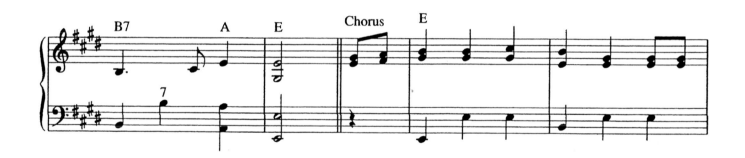

Aja Lejber Man

I'm a Labor Man

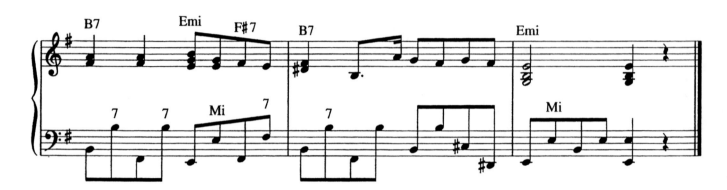

Opusceny Banik Z Wilks Barrock

The Lonely Miner

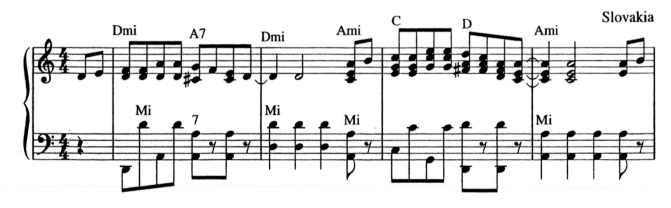

Ako Ay Pilipino

I am a Philipino

Philippines

Used by permission

6 (D)

O Emigrante
The Emigrant

Portugal

Pilipinas, Ang Bayan Ko
Philippines-My Native Land

Philippines

Used by permission

Izgnanik

The Exile

Bulgaria

Ein Männlein Steht in Walde

A Little Man Stands Midst the Trees

German

Amerikafeber

America Fever

Norway

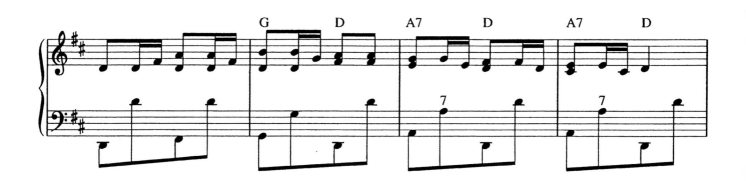

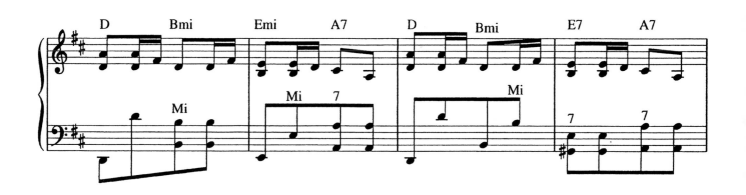

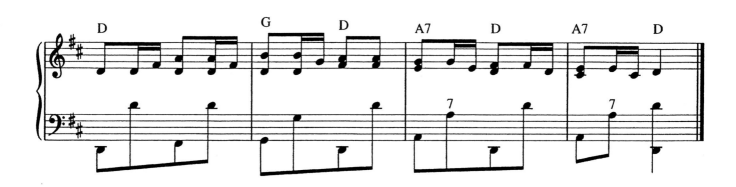

Proshchai, Rossiya
Farewell Russia

Russia

Used by permission

Duermete, Nino Lindo
Oh Sleep, My Little Baby

Mexico

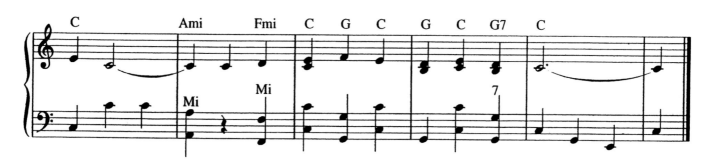

Il Sirio

The Sirio

Italy

Wilno Boys

Poland

Jak Jechalem Z Ameriki

America – I was Leaving

Poland

Zasvit' Mi, Ty Slunko Zlaté
Brightly Shine, O Golden Sunshine

Czech

Krasná Amerika

Pretty America

Czech

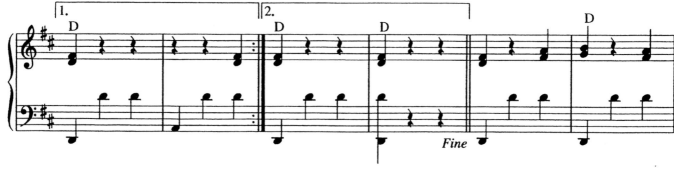

Fine

D.C.to 2nd Ending fine

Tarantella No. 3

Italy

A Briv Fun Amerike

A Letter from America

Jewish

Reisaavaisen Laulu Ameriikan

A Wanderer to America

Finland

Elämän Varrelta

In the Course of Life

Finland

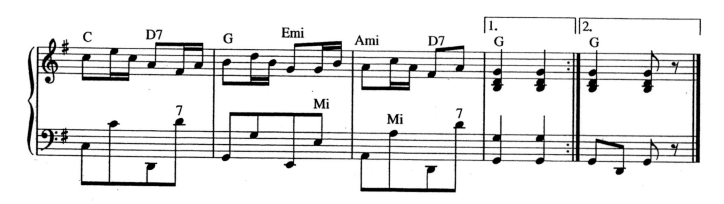

Boccherini's Menuetto

Italy

27

Mon Papa

My Papa

Voici' L' Hiver Bientôt Passé

Winter Will Soon be Passed Away

France

Fine

D.C al Fine

Le Carbbeau Et Le Renard

The Crow and the Fox

France - Canada

An Einen Auswanderer

To an Emigrant

Switzerland

Oleana

Norway

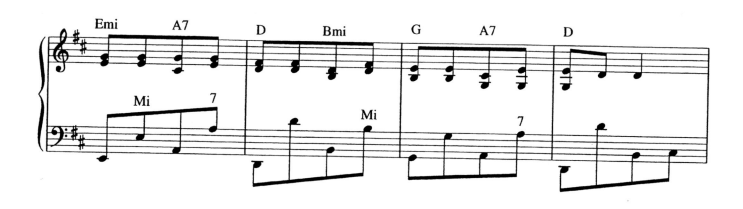

Chorus

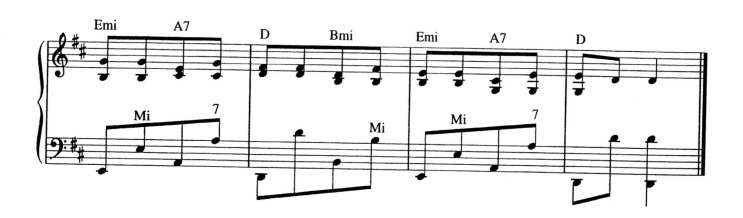

Dall' Italia Noi Siamo Partiti

When from Italy We Did Take Our Leave

Italy

Ny Vise Fra Udvandrene

New Song from the Emigrant

Denmark

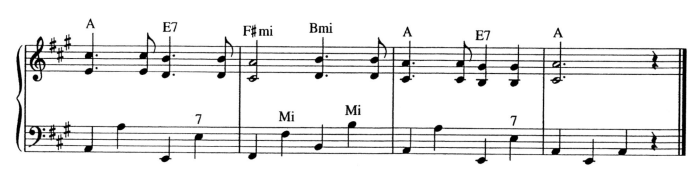

Auf Der Cimbria
On Board The Cimbria

Germany

Nun Ist Die Scheidestunde

Now is the Parting Hour

Germany

Song of the Holland Americans

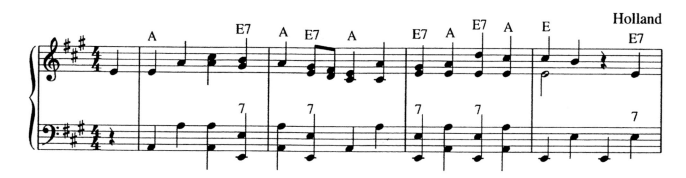

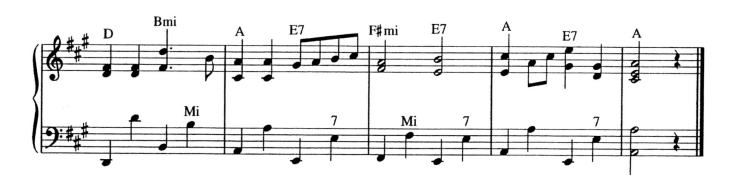

Bog Da Bie Koj Prv Pojde

God Punishes He Who Goes First

Cucul Tsutsul

O Yero Amerikanos

The Old American

Greece

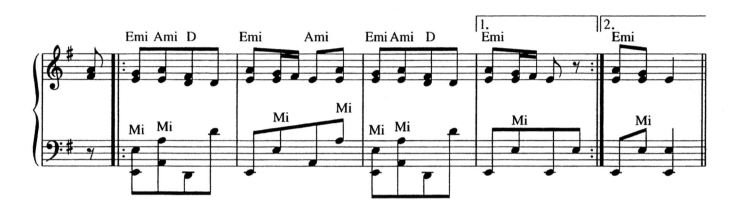

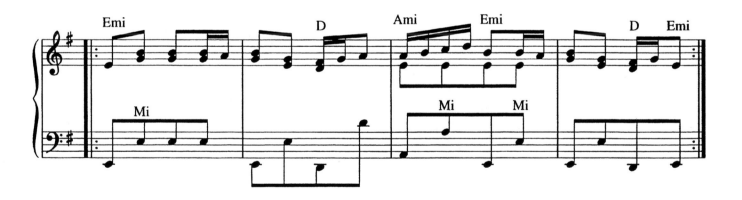

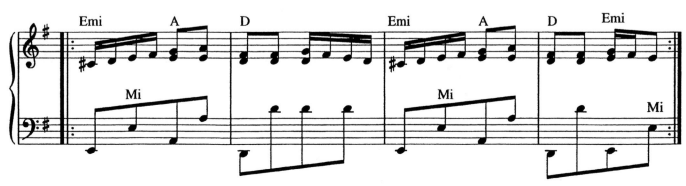

Fevgho Glikia
I'm Leaving Now

Greece

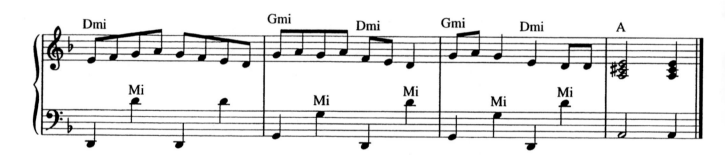

Tin Idha Ti Ksanthoula

I Saw My Dear Ksanthoula

Greece

Hazasodik A Tücsök

The Cricket's Wedding

Hungary

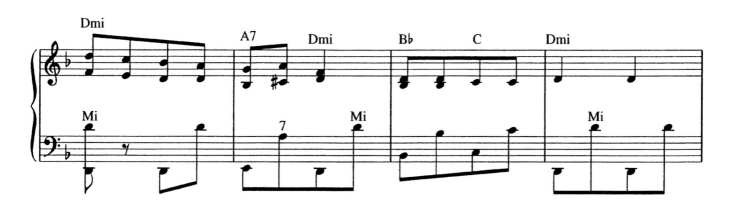

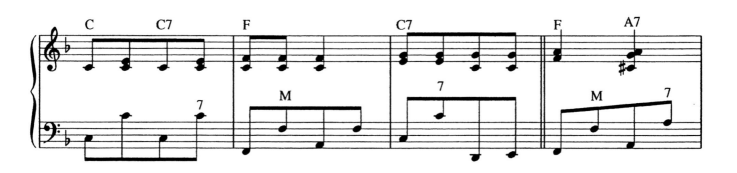

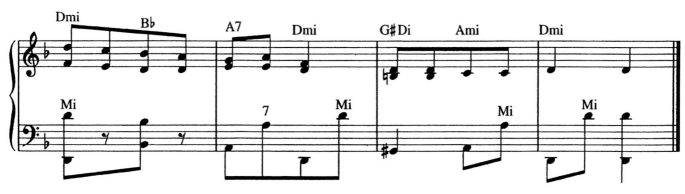

Langt Udi Skoven

Deep in the Forest

Denmark

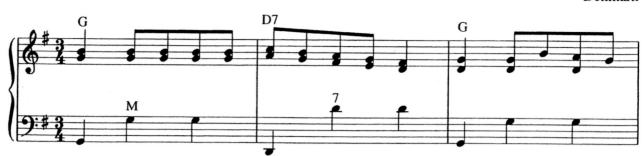

Sirotek

Czech

Kampuchea Aphaop
Poor Cambodia

Cambodia

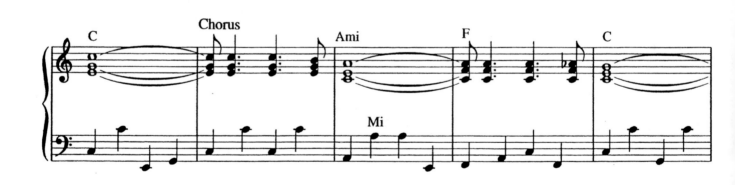

Mi Caballo Blanco

My White Horse

Chile

Oy Nema To Na Svetse

What a Most Delightful Life

Ukraine

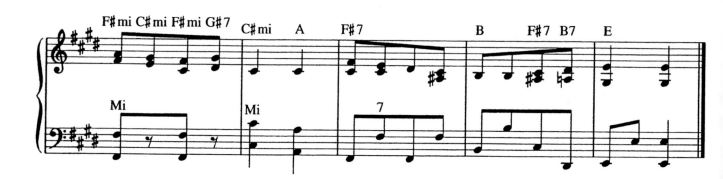

Moyi Mamtsia Doma

My Mother is at Home

Ukraine

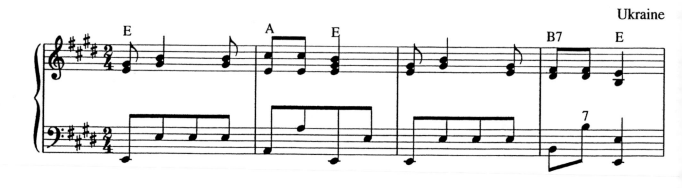

Kolumbus, Ich Hob Tsu Dir Gornit

Columbus, I Give You First Prize

Jewish

Aja Lejber Man

I'm a Labor Man

Slovakia

Hay Nazanem Yarer

Hey, My Dear Friends

Armenia

Zavičaju Mili Kraju

My Dear Homeland

Croatia

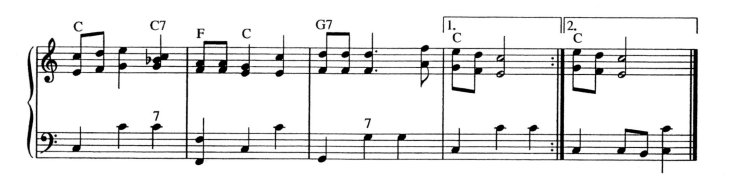

Elindultam Szép Hazámból

I Left My Nice Country

Hungary

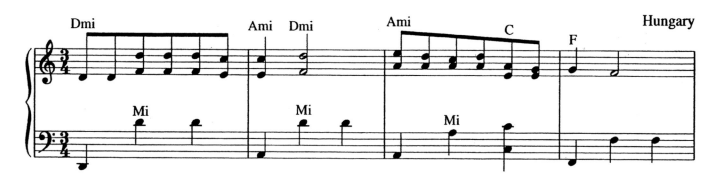

47

O Mraki

The Evening Bell

Slovenia

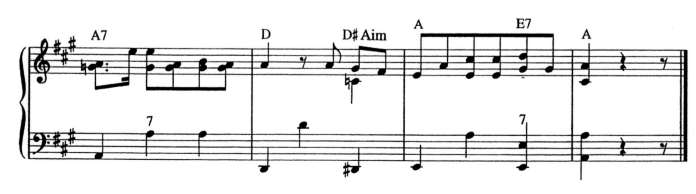

Lincoln-Visan
Lincoln Song

Sweden

Andante-Cantabile

Tschaikowsky

Melody in F

March Slav

Moderato

Tschaikowsky

Volga Boatmen's Song

Russian